GEORGE CATLIN Frontier Painter

by Jo Pitkin

HOUGHTON MIFFLIN BOSTON

For some, the American West is like a magnet. It draws people of all stripes: adventurers, schemers, drifters, the lazy and the industrious. George Catlin was one person who felt the pull of the West. By the time he was just twenty-six, he knew what he wanted to do with his life: to devote himself to studying the Native Americans on the western frontier, before white settlements changed them forever. But he wanted to do more than simply study them. He wanted to use his great skill as a painter to make a record of their faces, their rituals, their ways of finding food and shelter—their whole way of life.

When William Fisk painted this Catlin portrait in 1849, he included scenes from Catlin's works in the background.

Growing Up

In some ways, George Catlin made an unlikely adventurer. He was born on July 26, 1796, into a family with deep roots in the settled East. His father, Putnam Catlin, a well-educated lawyer, had served six years in the Continental Army during the American Revolution. Putnam Catlin made sure his sons were also well-educated, and George attended schools where he studied Latin and Greek, mathematics, and logic.

Although the family had strong ties to the prosperous East, they actually lived closer to the frontier of their day. For much of his childhood, George spent time hunting and fishing along the Susquehanna River Valley, in New York and Pennsylvania.

Living near the outer edge of settled lands, George and his family often had close contact with the Indians who still lived in the region. Before George was born, his mother, Polly, survived a massacre of white settlers in Pennsylvania's Wyoming Valley in 1778. For a time, Iroquois, Seneca, and Oneida warriors held her captive. This led to a life-long interest in Native American culture, and George often hunted for arrowheads in nearby woods and fields. One day, he came face to face with an Oneida hunter.

The hunter made Catlin a feathered bow and a tomahawk handle. He showed him how to throw a tomahawk. While practicing with friends, Catlin was cut by its sharp blade. For the rest of his life, he bore a long scar down his left cheek.

The Susquehanna River Valley as it looks today

Throughout his childhood, Catlin soaked up the lore of the frontier. Because his family lived near a popular westward trail, they often welcomed trappers, hunters, and migrating settlers to their home. Catlin's imagination was sparked by their tales of adventure, which stood in the sharpest contrast to the lessons he learned at school. Along with his mother's Indian-abduction tales, and the lore he learned from his Oneida friend, the stories of these visitors filled George's mind with images of the frontier.

When he was twenty-one, Catlin went to Litchfield, Connecticut, to study law at a prestigious school. He was a bright student, but not an especially eager one. Still, he passed his bar exam and began to practice law. He moved to Pennsylvania and set up a law office. But he wouldn't practice law for long.

While studying law, Catlin found that another interest began to draw his attention. He found his desire to practice law yielding to an interest in art. "Another and a stronger passion was getting the advantage of me—that for painting," he said of that time. He collected pens, inks, and other materials for his art, and brought them to his law office. While on the job as an attorney, he found time to paint or draw portraits of the judges, jurors, and defendants whom he observed in court. With no formal training in art, he found he was able to create remarkable likenesses of his subjects. After a few years, Catlin sold his law books and started on a new course. He was determined to pursue a career as a painter.

Becoming an Artist

Catlin moved to Philadelphia in 1821 and hung a sign by his door. It read, "George Catlin, Miniature Painter." In the days before photography, people had portraits painted when they wanted to have a picture of themselves or of a loved one. The portraits were like photos today. There were different kinds of portrait painters, including those who painted miniatures, like Catlin.

A Catlin miniature

He had taught himself to paint and had little time to develop a solid reputation as a painter. Yet Catlin's skill spoke for itself. Catlin knew that he could easily make a living as a portrait painter. His specialty was painting miniatures—tiny portraits—on ivory. Miniatures were very popular at the time, and business was strong for the young painter.

In Philadelphia, Catlin got to know some well-known artists. He visited Charles Willson Peale's museum, which featured portraits, scientific exhibits, and Native American artifacts. Peale's museum inspired Catlin to gather his own collection.

Catlin's reputation as a painter in Philadelphia grew quickly. Within one year, he exhibited four miniatures at the Pennsylvania Academy of Fine Arts. His works from this period include a miniature portrait of the famous leader, Sam Houston. This was one of the best portraits of Houston from that time. Just three years later, in 1824, he had attracted so much attention as a painter that he was elected to membership in the Academy. Catlin's dream of becoming a successful portrait painter was coming true.

For several years, his reputation as an artist grew. Yet the ambitious Catlin was not content in his new career. Then one day, he experienced something that shaped much of the rest of his life. He witnessed a visit to Philadelphia by a group of Indian men passing through on their way to Washington. He was deeply impressed by their dignity and colorful attire. Unlike others, he did not view them as exotic or odd. Instead, he saw their majesty.

Seeing this group revived Catlin's longtime fascination with American Indian life, and he quickly made a vow. From that time onward, he would do what he could to help the Native American peoples. In particular, he would make a record of their lives before their cultures were changed forever. Though he continued his work as a portrait painter for a time, his thoughts turned to the West. For the next two years he waited for an opportunity to travel to the frontier and paint the Indian tribes.

The task Catlin set for himself was grand enough to match his ambitions. "The history and customs of such a people, preserved by pictorial illustrations, are themes worthy the life-time of one man," he declared, "and nothing short of the loss of my life, shall prevent me from visiting their country, and of becoming their historian."

He would paint their faces—portraits were Catlin's specialty, after all. But he would also depict the events in their daily lives, such as ceremonies, rituals, dances, and games. In addition to using his paintings to record their customs, he would also create a collection of Indian artifacts. Catlin wished to make a permanent record of Native American life before it disappeared. The thought that their way of life might disappear without a trace filled Catlin with remorse. But ambition and desire drove him to complete the enormous goal he had set for himself.

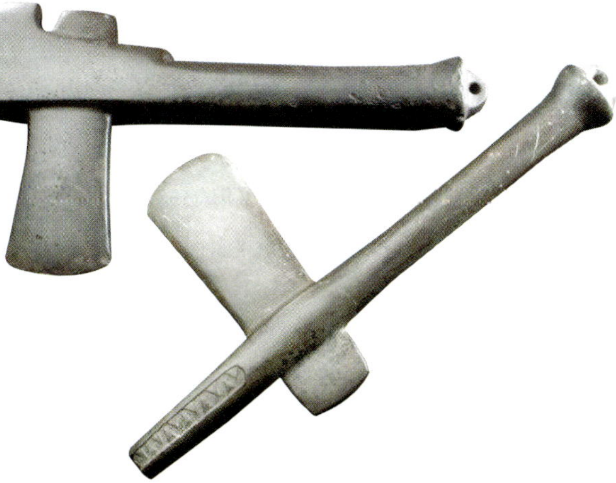

Artifacts, like these tomahawks, are one record of Native American history. Catlin wanted to create another record with his paintings.

The possibility that Indian cultures might be lost for good—the possibility that caused Catlin such sadness—was very real. Catlin's own parents had moved from the thoroughly settled lands of Connecticut, west toward the frontier. So did thousands of others. With every such move, the frontier pushed west, displacing more Native peoples. On a huge scale, the Indian Removal Act shows how this displacement worked. In 1830 the U.S. Congress passed the act and President Andrew Jackson signed it into law. As a result, many Indian groups were uprooted and driven far to the west.

This was a severe blow to the Cherokee, Choctaw, Chickasaw, and other tribes and nations. The Indian Removal Act fueled George Catlin's fears for the future of America's native population and added to the urgency of his mission.

"Go West, Young Man"

In 1830, George Catlin finally got his opportunity to go west. He packed his easel, paints, and brushes. Then, starting in western Pennsylvania, he set out on a long journey down the Ohio and Mississippi rivers. When he reached St. Louis, Missouri, he met William Clark. Clark had become the Governor of the Missouri Territory. He was also the Superintendent of Indian Affairs in the West.

Catlin couldn't have found a better person to introduce him to the West. In 1804, President Thomas Jefferson had sent William Clark and Meriwether Lewis on a famous scientific expedition. For two years, Lewis and Clark had explored the unknown territory between the Mississippi River and the Pacific Ocean. Here, they traveled thousands of miles and gathered important information about the people, plants, and animals of the West.

Catlin painted this portrait of William Clark, expedition leader and Governor of the Missouri Territory.

Now Clark agreed to help Catlin. He invited the artist to attend treaty councils with leaders of the Sioux, Missouri, Iowa, Omaha, and other tribes. At the meetings, representatives of the Sauk and Fox agreed to sell their lands to the United States government and move farther west.

Catlin's famous painting of Black Hawk, the Indian Leader

There was a famous exception to those agreeable Indian leaders. Catlin painted a famous portrait of the man, whose name was Black Hawk, a powerful leader of the Sauk and Fox peoples. Rather than give in to government demands and leave the land, Black Hawk led a bloody war against the United States and the white settlers of Illinois and Wisconsin. After his defeat, Black Hawk was captured and imprisoned. Catlin painted a portrait of him at a military barracks near St. Louis in 1832. Many people detested Black Hawk for the destruction his uprising caused. But Catlin portrayed Black Hawk in all his strength and dignity.

Painting in those military barracks was a far cry from painting in his old rooms back in Philadelphia. But it was further still from painting in the wilds of the West. Now Catlin headed out to the prairies and into the mountains beyond, where he would have little choice but to paint in the open land.

To do so, Catlin learned to work with only a handful of oil paint colors. On his back he carried a tin tube filled with rolled canvas. To work quickly, he would first sketch figures in brown paint on the canvas. Then he would apply thin strokes of color. When it was dry enough, Catlin rolled the painting up and carefully placed it back in the tube.

If he had time, Catlin filled in background details. If not, he finished painting in his studio when he returned east. To help remember what he had seen, Catlin carried a sketchbook and wrote detailed notes.

Steaming Up the Missouri

In the spring of 1832, Catlin ventured two thousand miles up the Missouri River. He traveled on the *Yellow Stone*, a new steamboat owned by the American Fur Company. He was delighted by the landscape of a "thousand hills and bluffs, and dales, and ravines." From the boat, he spotted buffalo, elk, antelope, wolves, and mountain goats. He commented, "It was to my eye, like a fairy-land."

Before Catlin arrived at the place where the Yellowstone River flowed into the Missouri, he went ashore on an expedition to Fort Pierre, in present-day South Dakota. There he painted traditional Sioux dances, such as the Bear Dance. He also observed the Sioux on a hunt and marveled at their skill at bringing down huge buffalo—on horseback, with only a bow and arrow. Catlin captured these scenes and many others with his paints. Today the paintings still provide a valuable glimpse into Indian life and culture of that time.

After a hazardous journey of three months, Catlin reached Fort Union, far up the Missouri in what is now Montana. There, he painted members of the Blackfoot and Crow tribes. After a Blackfoot chief was shot, Catlin recorded the ritual performed over the dying leader by a Blackfoot medicine man. Few people had ever witnessed ceremonies like these, and Catlin's paintings would fuel people's interest in the lore of the West and the customs of the Indians.

At the end of the summer, Catlin teamed up with two fur trappers who acted as guides. They traveled by canoe to friendly Mandan settlements. Spending a month with the Mandans, Catlin observed their daily life and became familiar with the customs and traditions of this small tribe. As with the Sioux, he was once again the first white man to witness and record many of the Mandan unique religious practices and ceremonies. However, his paintings of the Mandan were especially valuable. Most of them died soon after, in 1837, in a smallpox epidemic. Catlin was not only the first outsider to witness the Mandan rites, he was nearly the last.

In 1832, Catlin painted this portrait of an Indian chief in full dress.

During the next four years, Catlin repeated a pattern of visiting various tribes in spring, summer, and fall, and doing his sketching and note taking in the field. Then, in winter, he went home to the East and his wife, Clara. There he worked feverishly to finish his paintings. He was haunted by the thought that it would be only a matter of time before white settlers overran the remaining tribes as the frontier continued to roll west.

Riding to the Southwest

After exploring so much of the upper Missouri region, Catlin took a new direction when returning to the frontier in 1834. He was granted permission to ride with heavily armed soldiers on a mission to the Southwest. Riding a cream-colored mustang named Charley, he accompanied Colonel Henry Dodge and the U.S. Army's First Regiment of Mounted Dragoons. This expedition would also mark the first time the Army encountered the Comanches and Pawnees—two of the least-known tribes in North America.

It was also on this expedition that Catlin painted some of his most famous works. These paintings were inspired by the remarkable feats Catlin witnessed while he watched the Indians of the Southwestern plains. The Comanches were especially astounding horsemen, and Catlin wanted to capture them at their best. He wrote, "I am ready without hesitation to pronounce the Comanches the most extraordinary horsemen that I have seen and I doubt very much whether any people in the world can surpass them."

Catlin's *Comanche Giving Arrows to the Medicine Rock* depicts Comanche Indians practicing archery.

This journey to the Southwest was productive for Catlin, but also dangerous. A mysterious fever swept the regiment he traveled with, killing more than 200 of them. Catlin also fell deathly ill. Clinging to life, he was transported by wagon back to a U.S. Army fort. There he was treated in a hospital.

When he finally recovered, Catlin rode 500 miles, alone, to be reunited with his wife. They traveled to Florida and New Orleans for a winter of rest and recovery. But soon he was ready for another adventure.

Another journey west provided Catlin with more discoveries. During his earlier travels, Catlin had observed Native Americans smoking pipes at tribal councils and religious ceremonies. The pipes were made of red stone from a quarry in Minnesota. No white man had ever visited this mine. Catlin decided to find it.

A hostile band of Sioux warned Catlin not to trespass. But he refused to turn back. He visited the pipestone quarry in 1836. There he collected samples of the special stone used in making the pipes. It was later studied by a scientist in Boston who named it *catlinite*, in honor of Catlin.

Indian Gallery

In 1837, Catlin finally achieved his original goal. He had created more than four hundred oil paintings on American Indian themes. He had also collected thousands of Native American costumes, headdresses, drums, bows, and other objects. Now he arranged all his artifacts and paintings to create a display the public could view. During the next two years, he exhibited this Indian Gallery in American cities, including New York, Philadelphia, Washington, and Boston.

Although the public flocked to Catlin's exhibit, people's reactions were mixed. Before this time, few whites had seen any Native American people. Through his collection, Catlin depicted Native Americans as full human beings, different in their customs and cultures from whites, but still full of dignity and humanity. Some people refused to accept Catlin's point of view.

Nevertheless, Catlin expected more recognition for his collection of art and Indian artifacts. He hoped to sell it to the United States government. He thought it deserved to be preserved in a national museum. Perhaps alone, George Catlin understood the enormous amount of work that went into creating the collection and the bounty of information it held about Native American life.

Catlin offered his "gallery" to the government for $150,000, but the government declined. Smarting from this rejection, Catlin decided to take his collection to Europe. He hoped that if European buyers showed interest in his collection, the United States government might realize how valuable the gallery was.

In 1839, Catlin sailed for England with eight tons of paintings and artifacts. In London's Egyptian Hall, he exhibited more than four hundred portraits, landscapes, and scenes of Native American life. In the center of the room, he placed thousands of weapons, costumes, utensils, and other items around a white tipi.

Catlin's *Comanche War Party, Mounted on Wild Comanche Horses*

After setting up the display, Catlin became its main host and promoter. By day he worked at Egyptian Hall answering visitors' questions. By night, he gave lectures on the West and its Indian tribes. Catlin's tireless efforts to educate people about Native Americans earned him fame and respect. His efforts also helped stoke interest in the American West among the English, who were fascinated by his tales.

Reversal of Fortune

During the next five years, Catlin continued exhibiting his paintings and artifacts in England. He met Queen Victoria and other members of the royal family. He published a popular account of his experiences: *Letters and Notes of the Manners, Customs, and Condition of the North American Indians.* To keep attracting people's interest, Catlin added live shows to his Indian Gallery. He hired Native Americans to perform dances and ride horses. But gradually the public lost interest in visiting his gallery and Catlin began to lose money.

In 1845, Catlin moved his gallery to France. At first, the French exhibition was a huge success, as it had been in England. But the Native Americans in Catlin's show grew homesick and sailed home. As the popularity of his show declined and his debts mounted, Catlin himself decided to leave Europe.

A wealthy American merchant finally bought Catlin's gallery and had it shipped to Philadelphia from France.

After an absence of thirty-two years, Catlin returned to the United States in 1871. Worried about the fate of his life's work, Catlin wrote Congress one last time. Again the government refused to buy his collection, although it now included more than one thousand paintings and sketches. Defeated, Catlin fell into serious illness. Among his last words, he asked: "What will happen to my gallery?" He died in New Jersey on December 23, 1872.

Catlin's Legacy

What did happen to Catlin's Indian Gallery? For more than thirty years, it was stored in the dingy basement of a Philadelphia factory. Mice, moths, fire, and water damaged it. Some of the artifacts and paintings were completely destroyed. Fortunately, many of Catlin's early paintings of Native Americans survived. They were eventually cleaned and restored. Seven years after his death, what remained of his original collection was donated to the Smithsonian Institution.

Catlin left an important legacy of paintings and eyewitness accounts that provide a view of Native American life in the 1800s. Catlin gained the trust of the painting subjects, lived among them, and provided an interpretation of their ways. While those customs took hundreds, even thousands of years to develop, they were almost destroyed in a few short decades. George Catlin had the rare fortune to witness and record those customs in the years just before change overwhelmed them.

Visitors today can still see part of Catlin's original collection at the Smithsonian Institution.

In the long years after he chose his life's work, George Catlin never forgot his mission. He did not manage to observe and document the culture of every North American tribe, as he had hoped to do. But—although he never knew it—he did help to educate future generations about "the living manners, customs, and character of a people who were rapidly passing away from the face of the earth—a dying nation who had no historians or biographers of their own."

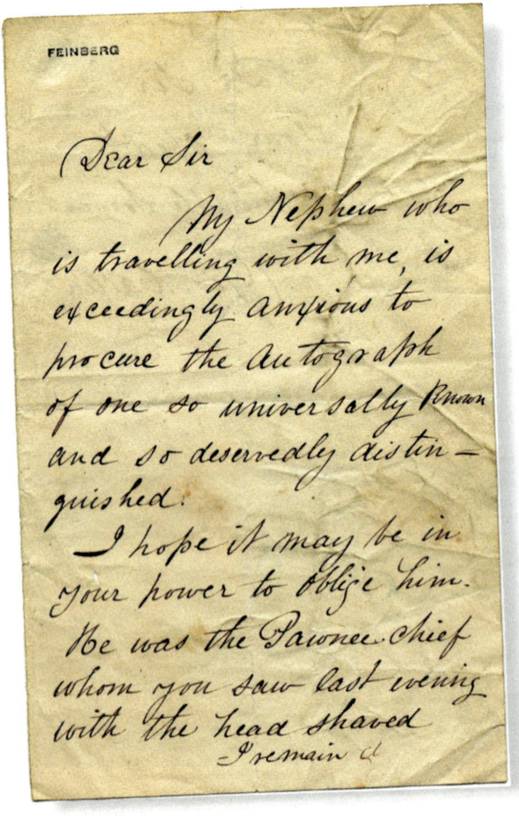
FEINBERG

Dear Sir

My Nephew who is travelling with me, is exceedingly anxious to procure the Autograph of one so universally known and so deservedly distinguished.

I hope it may be in your power to oblige him.
He was the Pawnee chief whom you saw last evening with the head shaved

I remain &c

A letter from George Catlin from the 1850s